ORIGAMI ANIMALS

DOVER PUBLICATIONS, INC., MINEOLA, NEW YORK

Copyright

Bibliographical Note

Origami Animals, first published by Dover Publications, Inc., in 2019, is a new English translation of the work originally published by NuiNui, Switzerland, in 2019.

Translation from the Italian: Martin Maguire

International Standard Book Number

ISBN-13: 978-0-486-84199-1
ISBN-10: 0-486-84199-5

Manufactured in China
84199501
www.doverpublications.com
2 4 6 8 10 9 7 5 3 1
2019

Text and diagrams

Mila Bertinetti Montevecchi

Rita Foelker

Nick Robinson

Marc Kirschenbaum

• •

Photographs

Dario Canova

Araldo De Luca

Nick Robinson

Céline Ribordy

Contents

Instructions   *page* 5

Techniques   *page* 6

Little Bird - Rita Foelker   *page* 12

Caterpillar - Rita Foelker   *page* 16

9-Fold Butterfly - Lee Armstrong   *page* 20

Crab - Mila Bertinetti Montevecchi   *page* 24

Scottie Dog - Robert Neale   *page* 30

Cat - Traditional   *page* 34

Turtle - Marc Kirschenbaum   *page* 42

Owl - Marc Kirschenbaum   *page* 48

Instructions

Choosing paper

Square-shaped sheets of paper are usually used when creating origami models. Once you run out of the enclosed paper, you may purchase more in hobby shops or on the Internet.

- The best option would be purchasing large sheets of paper and then sizing them down to smaller square dimensions. This provides remarkable savings.
- Usually origami paper is two-toned: colored on one side and white on the other.
- You may use sheets of paper with different patterns and colors when creating the origami models in this book.
- Origami paper with a wide variety of patterns may be found for sale: choose the kind that is best suited to the origami model that you have chosen.
- We suggest trying your hand with less expensive paper before working on the final origami with your finest paper.

How to fold

- Arrange the sheet of paper on a hard, smooth surface, possibly a well-illuminated table, and make sure you have enough space for comfortable elbow movement.
- Always remember that paper is a very sensitive material and that once you make a fold, it is practically impossible to eliminate all traces of the fold.
- Prepare every fold with extreme care: take all the time you need, concentrate on your work, and make sure that the paper is perfectly arranged on the work surface.
- When you are ready, take the lower edge of the paper and slowly lift it to the upper edge, always keeping the sheet of paper steady on the work surface with your other hand.
- When the two edges are perfectly aligned, start flattening the folds by delicately pressing them with a light movement in the direction of the fold.
- Finally complete the fold: in order to have a distinct and well-defined finish, press the edge with the back of your fingernail (usually using the thumb).
- Many people prefer folding origami paper outward rather than inward, so that their hands do not get in the way.

Techniques

Name of the symbol	Aspects of the symbol	Application of the symbol	Result of the application
Valley fold			
Valley and unfold			
Mountain fold			
Mountain and unfold			
Repeat the crease once, twice, three times, etc.			

Name of the symbol	Aspects of the symbol	Application of the symbol	Result of the application
Fold to dotted line	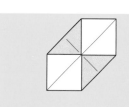		
Inside reverse	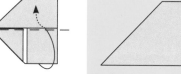		
Hidden edges (to X-rays)			
Turn over		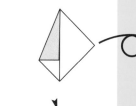	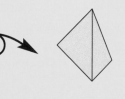
Push, press, turn inside	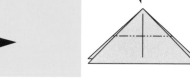		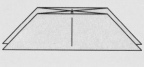

Name of the symbol	Aspects of the symbol	Application of the symbol	Result of the application

Rotate the origami in a different direction

Fold the bisector of a corner

Crimp

Symmetrical crimp

Unfold one or more folds, one or more layers

Name of the symbol	Aspects of the symbol	Application of the symbol	Result of the application
Enlarged origami			
Reduced origami			
Fold at 90°	90°	90°	
Bulge			
Transition to three-dimensional	3D	3D 90° 90°	

Little Bird

Rita Foelker

This little bird is not able to fly yet and is keeping warm in its nest: it is the perfect symbol for the section dedicated to the protection of nature. Even folding a simple sheet of paper, which will then come to life as if by magic, is a way to launch a message of confidence in humanity's willingness to respect the world around us.

Use a triangular sheet of paper, cutting the square paper in two as shown.

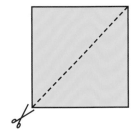

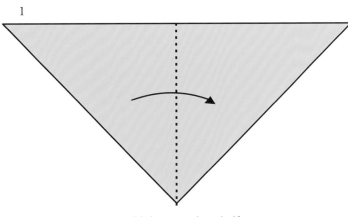

1. Fold the triangle in half.

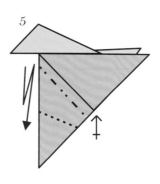

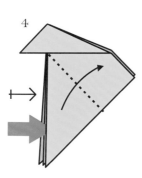

5. Make a zigzag fold to hide part of the paper and leave only a foot showing; repeat the operation for the reverse side.

4. Raise the lower tip and fold it to create a wing; repeat the operation for the reverse side.

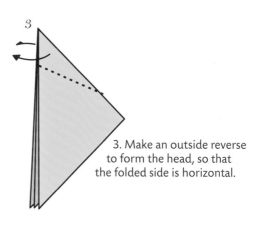

3. Make an outside reverse to form the head, so that the folded side is horizontal.

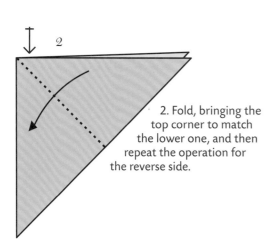

2. Fold, bringing the top corner to match the lower one, and then repeat the operation for the reverse side.

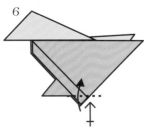

6. Raise the small lower triangle slightly: you will need this to make the bird stand upright; repeat the operation for the reverse side.

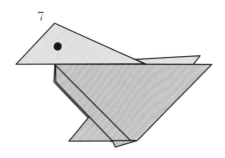

7. The little bird is ready! Now you can draw its eyes.

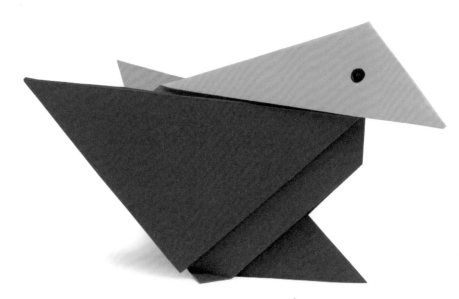

Caterpillar

Rita Foelker

The butterfly goes through three stages before it becomes what it is meant to be: egg, caterpillar, and pupa. The mother deposits the eggs on leaves for it to eat at the time of its hatching: until it turns into a pupa, the caterpillar will devour lots and lots!

1

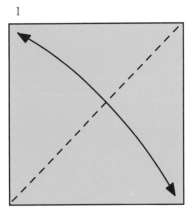

1. Place the plain side of the sheet facing you. Fold the sheet in half, joining the corners, and reopen.

2

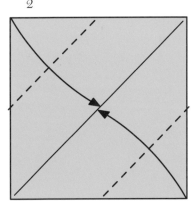

2. Fold the corners toward the center.

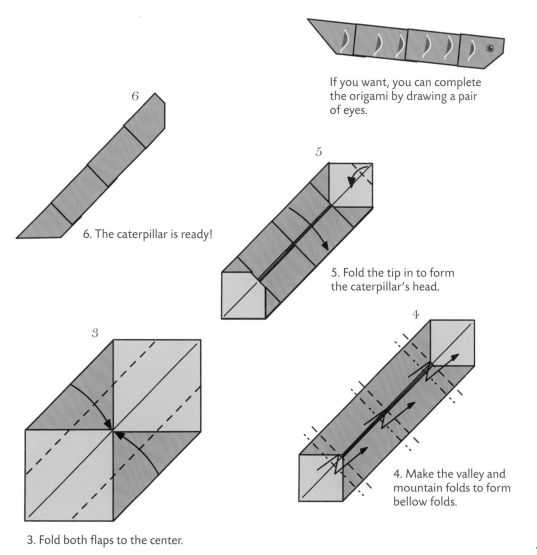

If you want, you can complete the origami by drawing a pair of eyes.

6. The caterpillar is ready!

5. Fold the tip in to form the caterpillar's head.

4. Make the valley and mountain folds to form bellow folds.

3. Fold both flaps to the center.

17

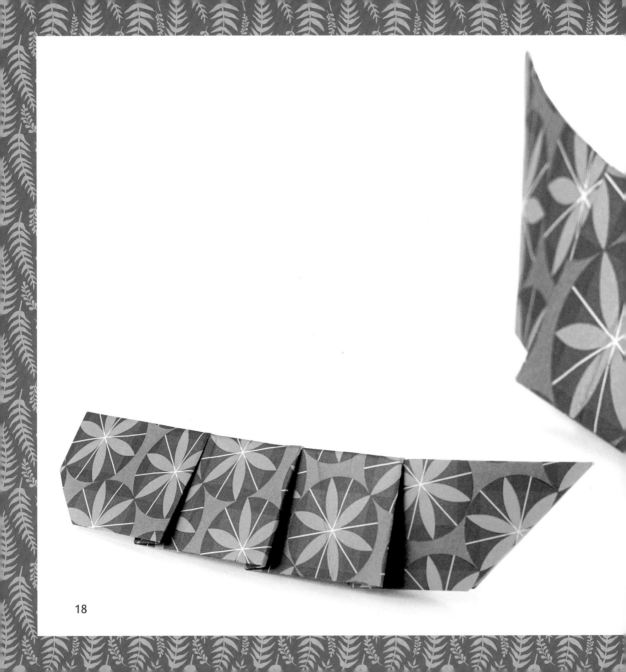

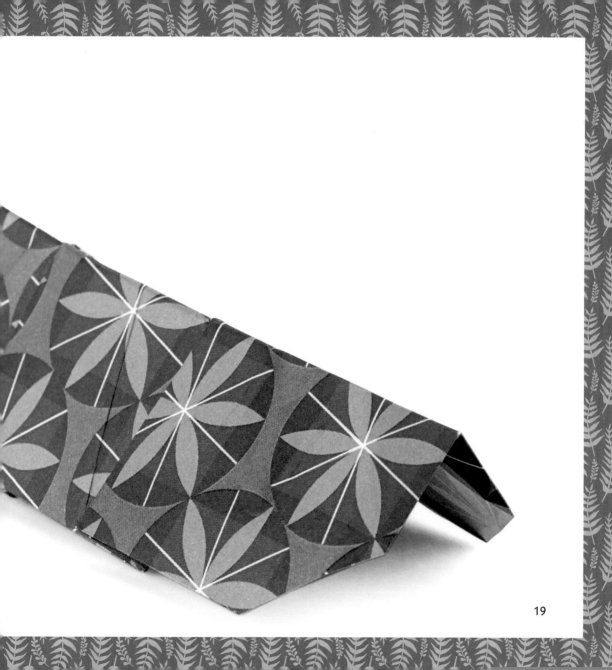

9-Fold Butterfly

Lee Armstrong

Lee developed this design to illustrate how, in step 1, there are an infinite number of ways to divide a square equally in half. If you are happy with a 2D result, disregard the last two steps, for a 7-fold butterfly!

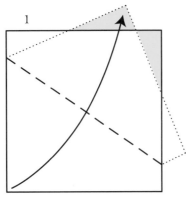

1. White side up, fold the lower left corner to match the dotted line. The idea is to make the two shaded areas identical. Rotate the paper slightly.

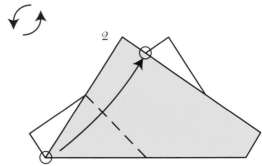

2. Fold so the circled corners meet.

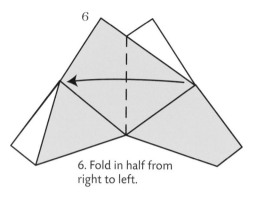

6. Fold in half from right to left.

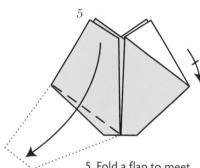

5. Fold a flap to meet the dotted line. Repeat on the right.

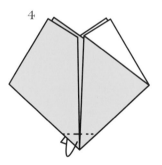

4. Fold the lower corner behind.

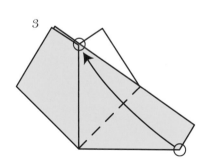

3. Repeat the last step on the right.

21

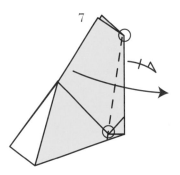

7. Fold one wing to the right between the circled points. Repeat on the underside (so this counts as two steps!). Rotate the model 180 degrees.

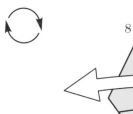

8. Open out into 3D.

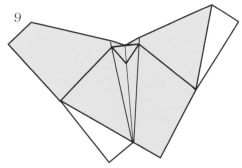

9. The 9-Fold Butterfly is finished.

Crab

Mila Bertinetti Montevecchi

Crabs are very shy animals: they tend to emerge at night and move sideways. Most live on rocks in the sea, but there are also freshwater crabs. All have two big claws, like powerful pincers, with which they capture their food. The world's largest crab lives in Japan and can open its claws as wide as ten feet, but it is rarely seen.

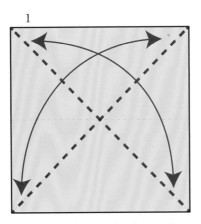

1. Fold in half along the diagonals and reopen.

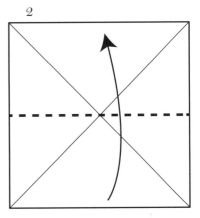

2. Fold the sheet in half upward.

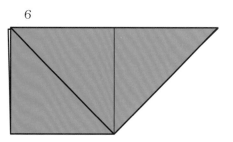

6. Turn the model over.

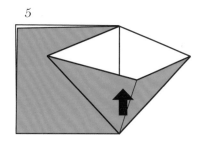

5. Squash the paper.

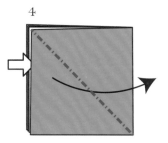

4. Open only the first layer to the right with a backward fold.

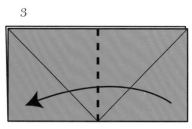

3. Fold in half to the left.

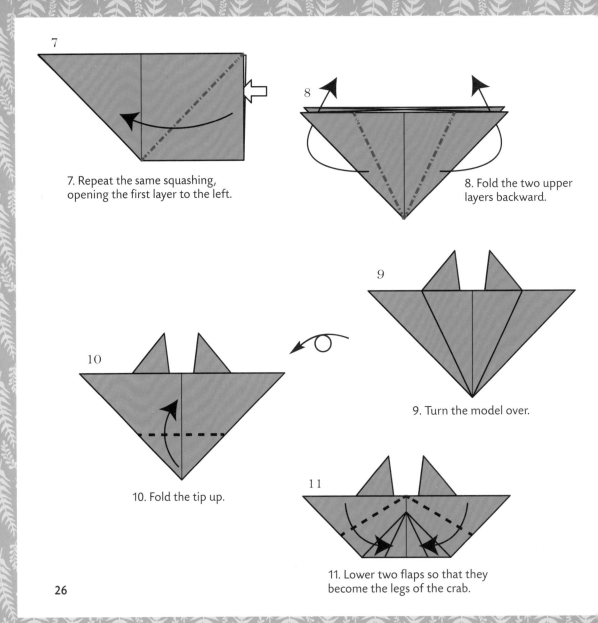

7. Repeat the same squashing, opening the first layer to the left.

8. Fold the two upper layers backward.

9. Turn the model over.

10. Fold the tip up.

11. Lower two flaps so that they become the legs of the crab.

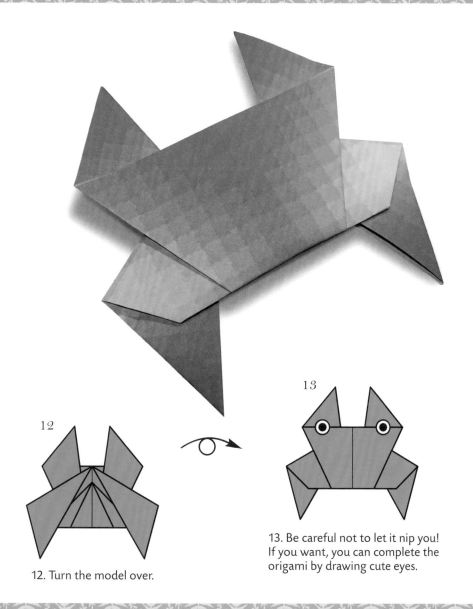

12. Turn the model over.

13. Be careful not to let it nip you! If you want, you can complete the origami by drawing cute eyes.

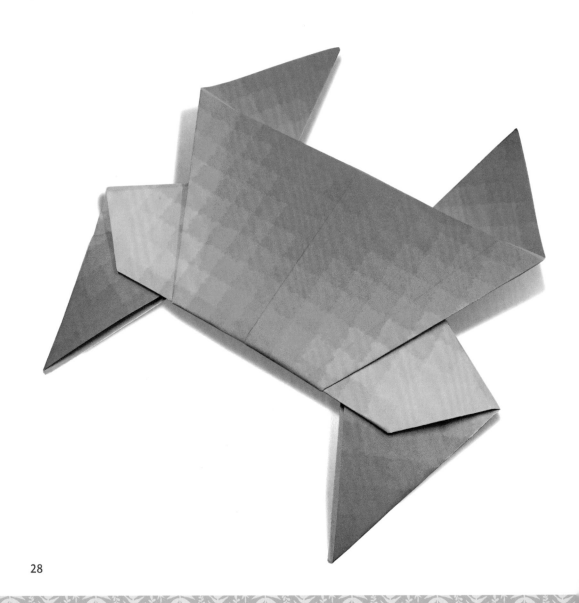

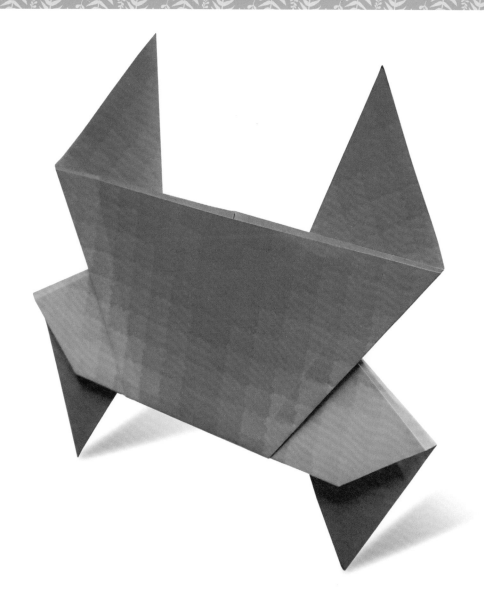

Scottie Dog

Robert Neale

An unusual folding sequence produces a charming result.

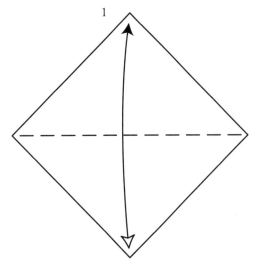

1. White side up, fold in half, crease and unfold.

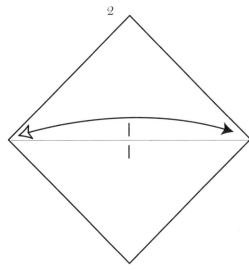

2. Pinch the center of the diagonal.

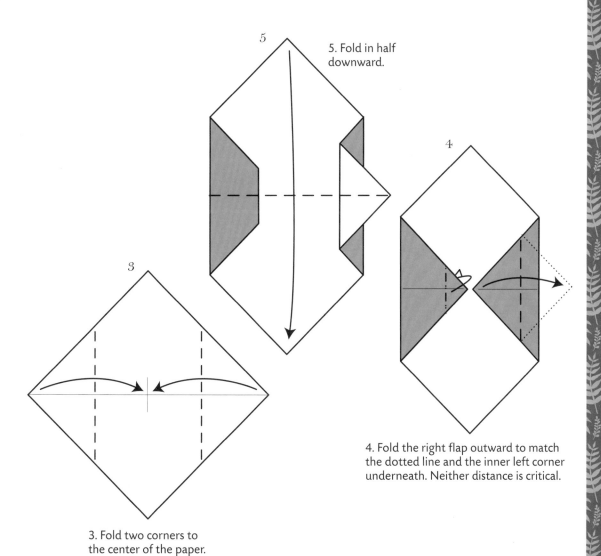

5. Fold in half downward.

4. Fold the right flap outward to match the dotted line and the inner left corner underneath. Neither distance is critical.

3. Fold two corners to the center of the paper.

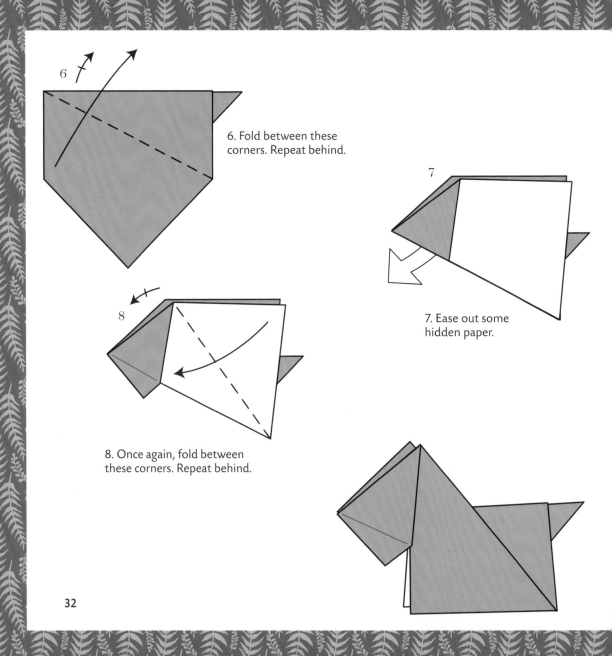

6. Fold between these corners. Repeat behind.

7. Ease out some hidden paper.

8. Once again, fold between these corners. Repeat behind.

32

Cat

Traditional

A simple folding sequence allows you to make many different—shaped cats. The two parts need different—sized papers; see page 35.

THE HEAD

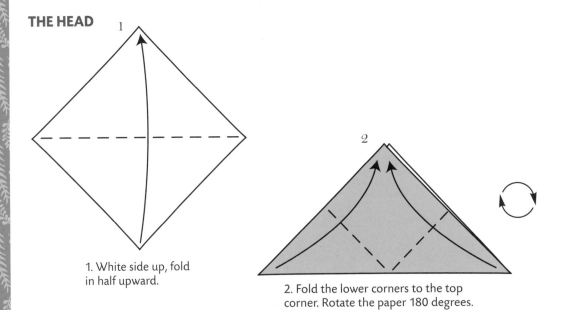

1. White side up, fold in half upward.

2. Fold the lower corners to the top corner. Rotate the paper 180 degrees.

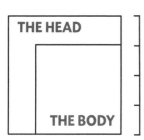

THE HEAD

THE BODY

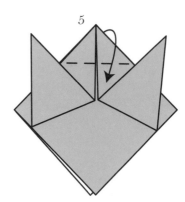

5. Fold the upper corner down between the ears.

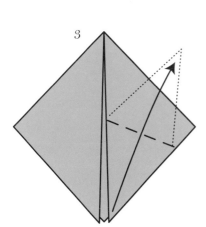

3. Fold a corner up to match the dotted lines, or wherever you want!

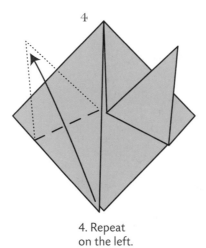

4. Repeat on the left.

35

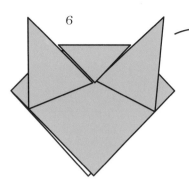

6. This is the result.
Turn the model over.

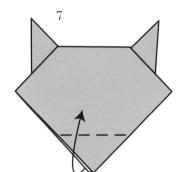

7. Fold up both layers.

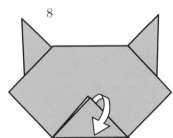

8. Ease the white
flap out and tuck the
colored edge under it.

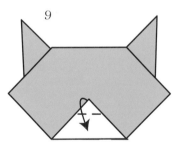

9. Fold the inner corner
down to create the
perfect nose.

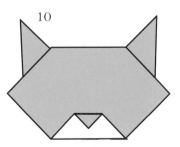

10. The head
is complete.

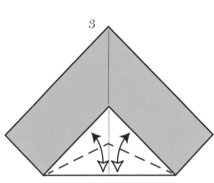

3. Fold the upper white edges to the lower, creasing only as far as the center.

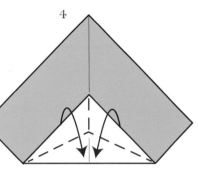

4. Make these three creases at the same time, forming a central point.

THE BODY

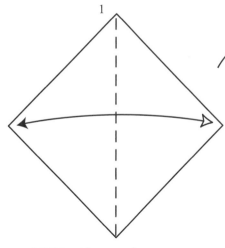

1. White side upward, crease and unfold a diagonal. Turn the paper over.

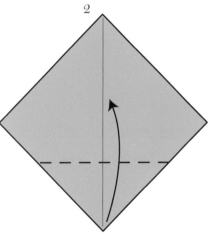

2. Fold about one third upward.

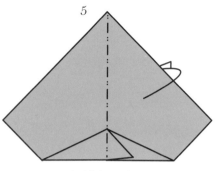

5. Fold the right half behind.

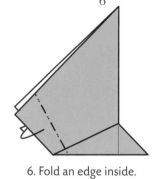

6. Fold an edge inside.

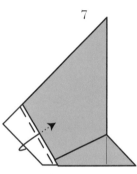

7. Fold the lower edge in as well. Rotate the paper.

8. The body is complete.

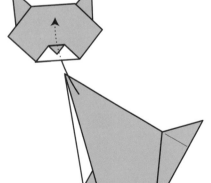

9. Slide the point of the body inside the layers of the head. It should stay in place, but you can always use a little glue.

Turtle

Marc Kirschenbaum

Turtles can be different sizes: from 1–2 inches, up to 7–10 feet for the largest species. There are many species of turtle, just as there are many origami variants. This model, in particular, looks like a small red-eared turtle, originally from North America, but present today all over the world; its favorite habitats are lakes, ponds, and slow-moving rivers, and muddy water with plenty of aquatic plants.

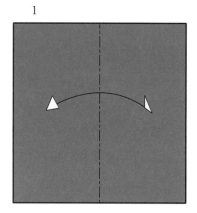

1. Precrease with a mountain fold.

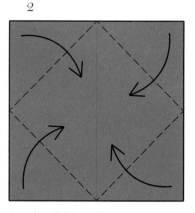

2. Valley fold the four corners to the center.

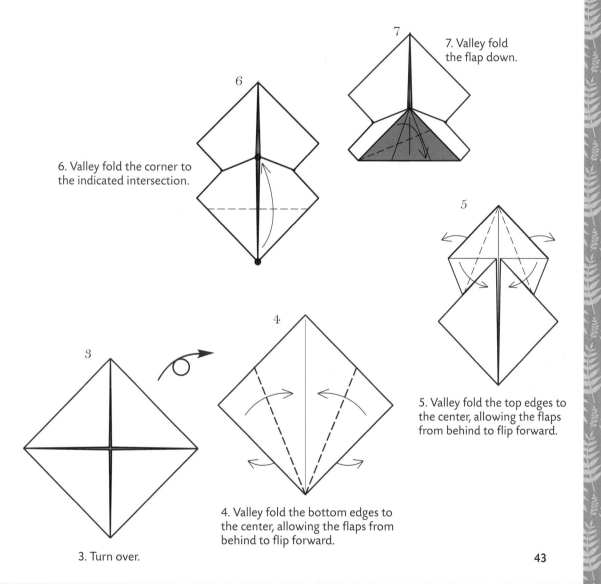

7. Valley fold the flap down.

6. Valley fold the corner to the indicated intersection.

5. Valley fold the top edges to the center, allowing the flaps from behind to flip forward.

4. Valley fold the bottom edges to the center, allowing the flaps from behind to flip forward.

3. Turn over.

43

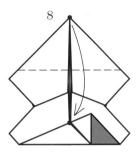

8. Valley fold the corner to the indicated intersection.

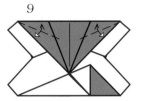

9. Precrease along the angle bisectors.

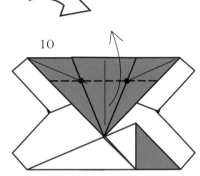

10. Valley fold up through the indicated intersections.

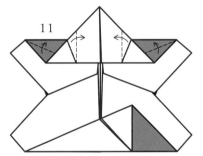

11. Swivel the sides inward.

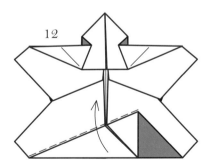

12. Swing the bottom flap up.

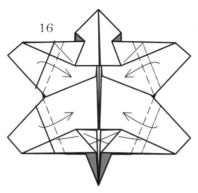

16. Pleat the four flaps inward.

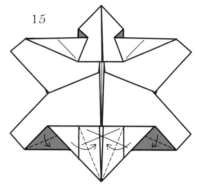

15. Swivel the sides inward.

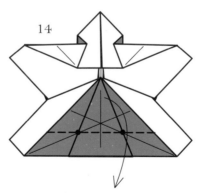

14. Valley fold down through
the indicated intersections.

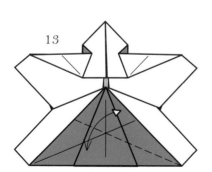

13. Precrease along the angle
bisector.

45

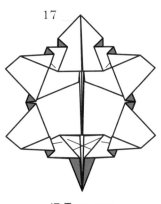

17

17. Turn over.

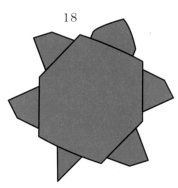

18

18. Completed Turtle.

Owl

Marc Kirschenbaum

As you will see, all you need to make this model are simple valley and mountain folds. The Englishman John Smith called this type of folding "Pureland." Despite its simplicity, the model has small ears that give it character.

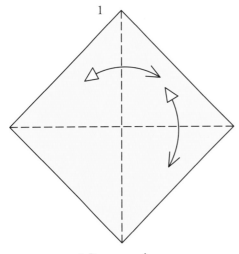

1. Precrease along the diagonals.

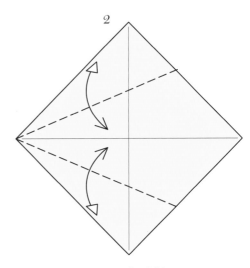

2. Precrease by folding the sides to the center.

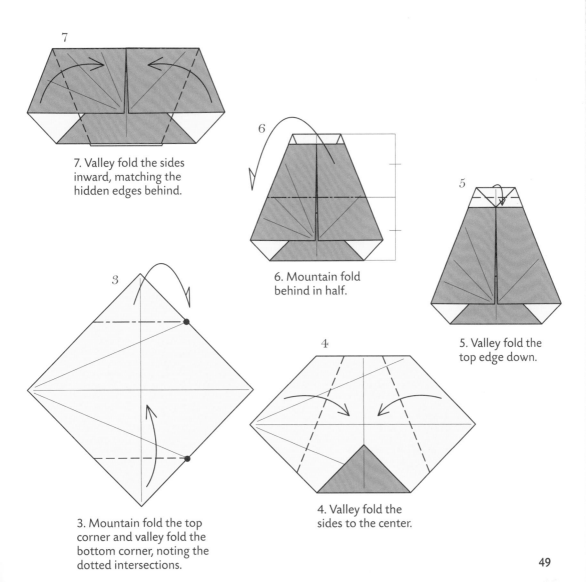

7. Valley fold the sides inward, matching the hidden edges behind.

6. Mountain fold behind in half.

5. Valley fold the top edge down.

3. Mountain fold the top corner and valley fold the bottom corner, noting the dotted intersections.

4. Valley fold the sides to the center.

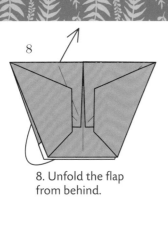

8. Unfold the flap from behind.

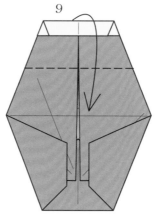

9. Valley fold toward the center crease.

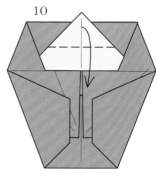

10. Valley fold the corner a little bit past the edge.

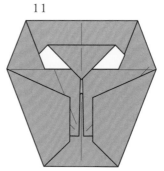

11. Turn over.

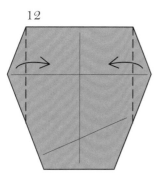

12. Valley fold the sides inward.

16. Completed Owl.

15. Turn over.

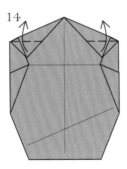

14. Valley fold the corners up.

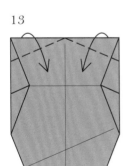

13. Valley fold the corners down.

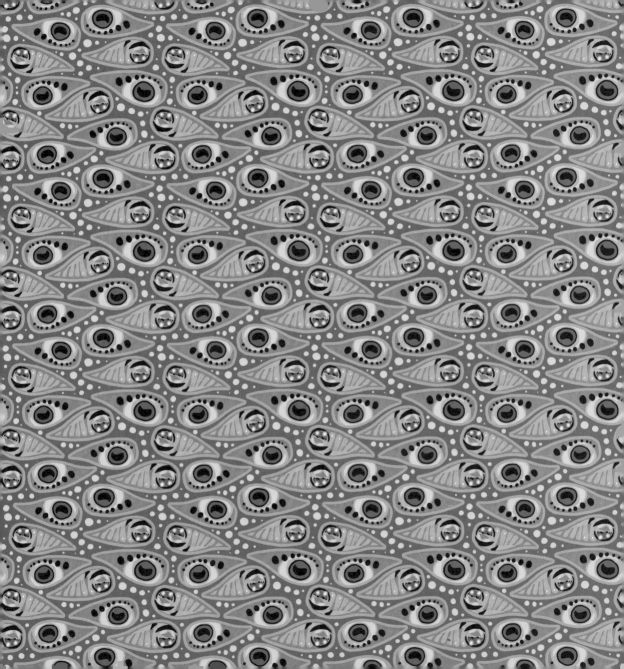

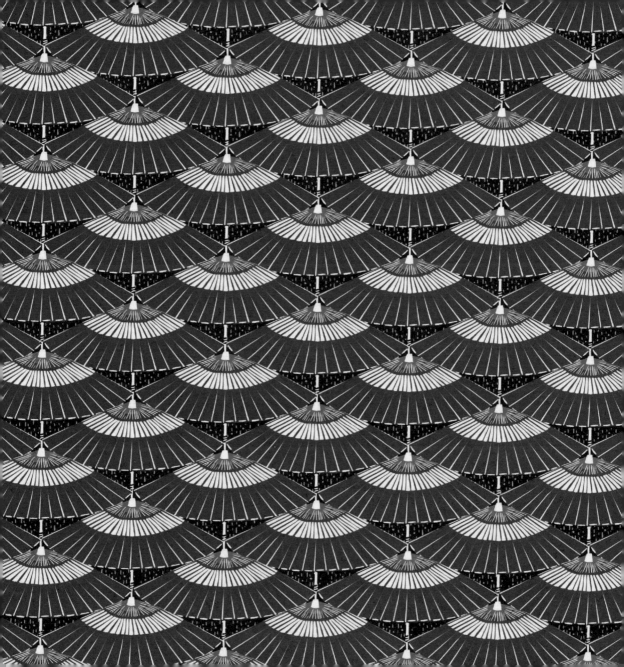

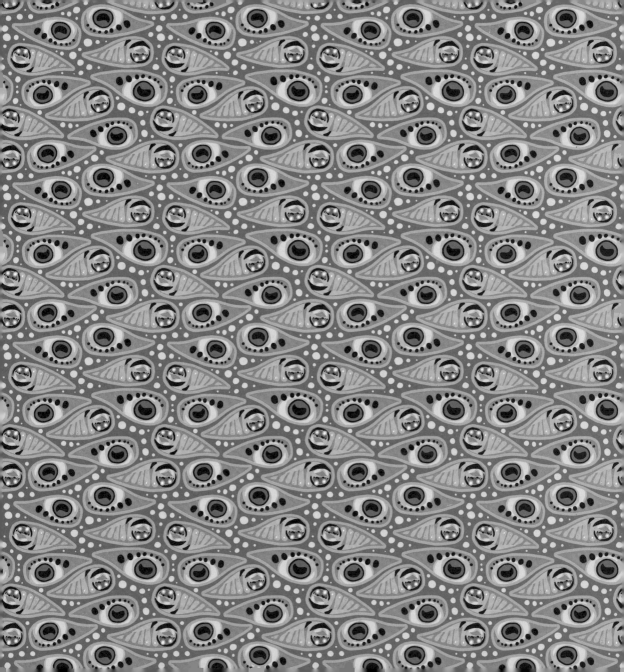

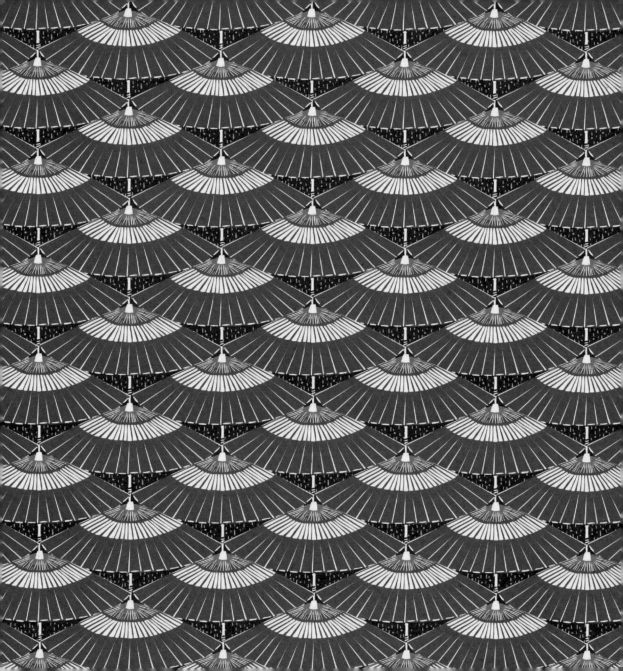

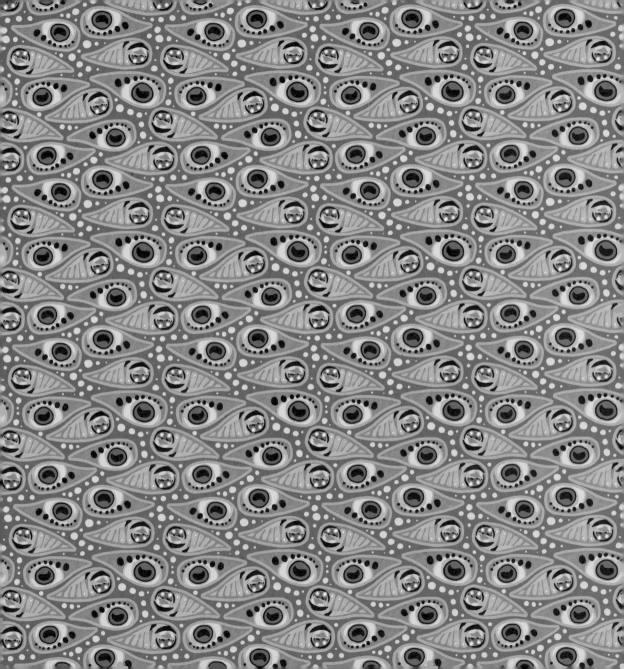

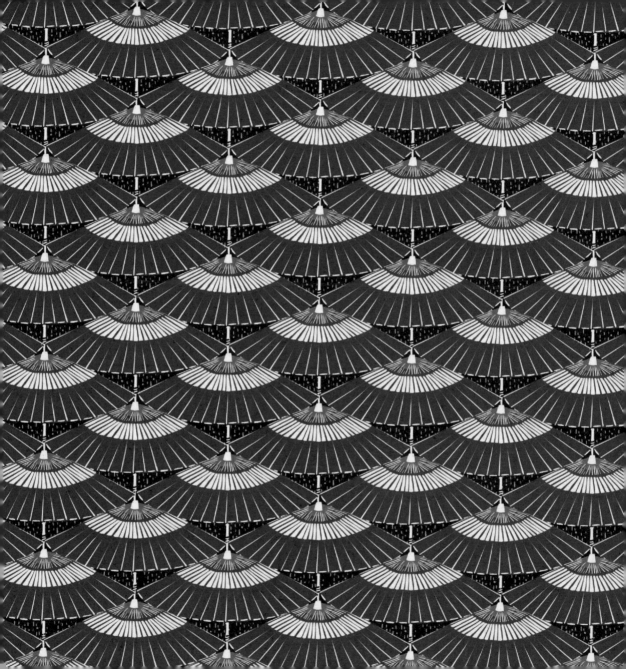

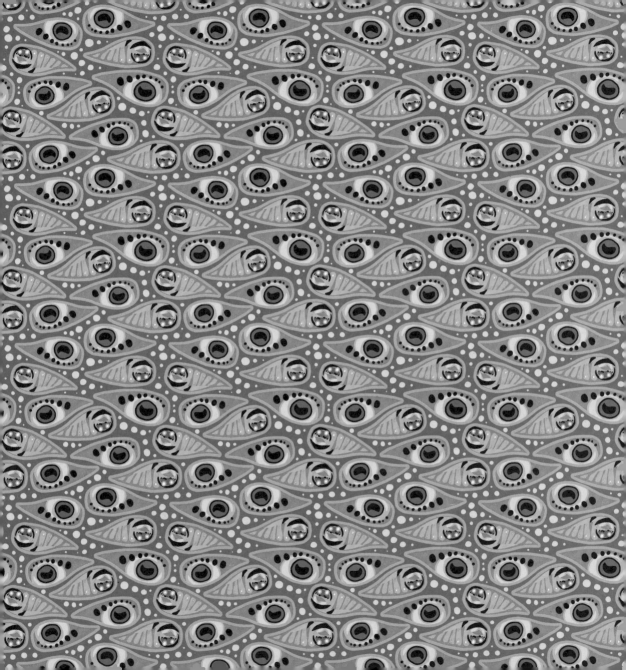

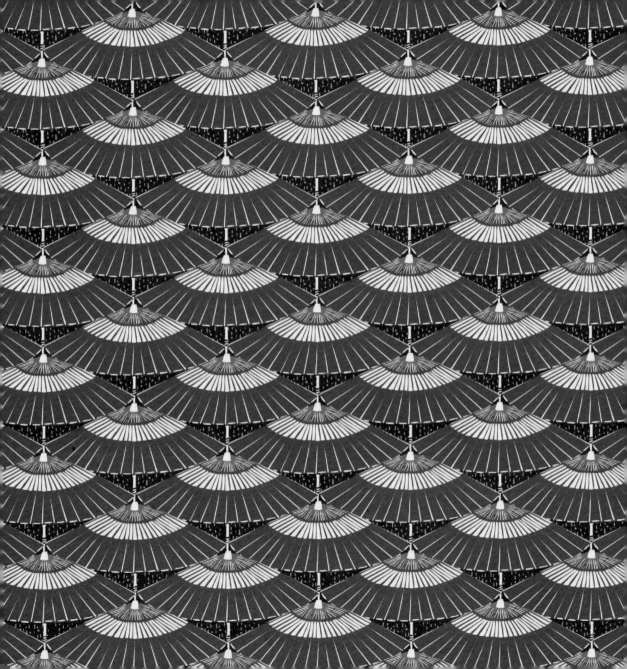

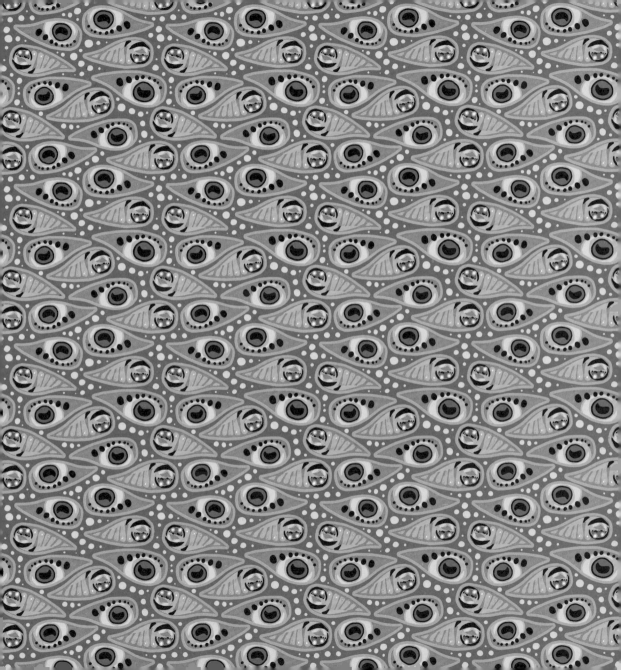

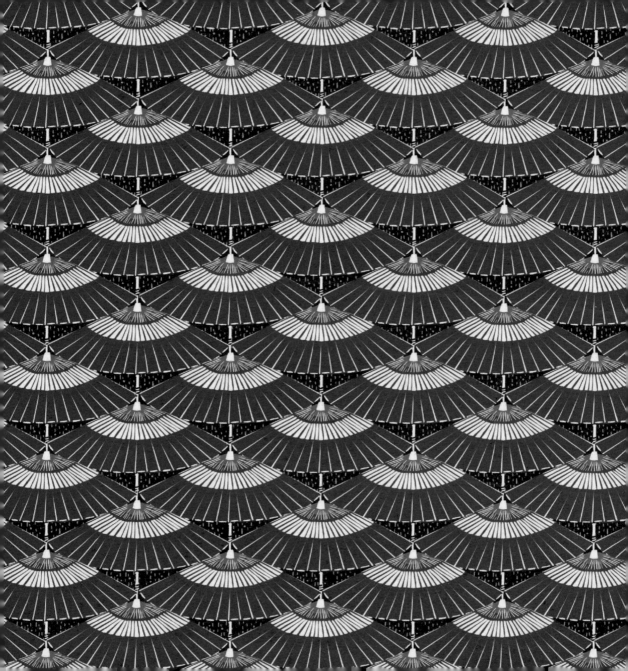